Valparaiso

A PLAY IN TWO ACTS

Don DeLillo

SCRIBNER

SCRIBNER
1230 Avenue of the Americas
New York, NY 10020

Inquiries concerning performance rights in *Valparaiso*
should be addressed to The Gersh Agency, New York, NY

Valparaiso received its first performance
on January 29, 1999, directed by David Wheeler
at the American Repertory Theatre, Cambridge,
Massachusetts, Artistic Director Robert Brustein,
Managing Director Robert J. Orchard.

DESIGNED BY ERICH HOBBING
Manufactured in the United States of America

1   3   5   7   9   10   8 6   4   2

Library of Congress Cataloging-in-Publication Data
is available.

ISBN 0-684-86421-5

To Frank Lentricchia

Michael Majeski	The Interviewers
Livia Majeski	The Camera Crew
Delfina Treadwell	The Chorus
Teddy Hodell	

Two actors, one male, one female, play all the Interviewers in Act One.

The three members of the Camera Crew double as Chorus.

Act One

Living room of the Majeski house. A large uncluttered space. The decorative scheme is showroom bright and somewhat generic—not sterile so much as self-conscious, like a representative room installed in an art museum.

In several scenes a sector of this playing area functions as office space or as interview space in a broadcast studio.

Scene 1

The living room. Livia sits on an exercise bike, facing down-stage. She looks into the middle distance, pedaling steadily.

Lights slowly down.

There is a deep pulse of image and sound. A videotape is projected on the back wall and adjacent furniture. It shows a single image, a high-angle shot of a man in a tightly confined space. There is a plastic bag on his head, fastened about the neck. He is seated, a forearm braced against the wall to either side of him. The plastic is thick and frosted, obscuring the man's features.

The tape is crude and marked by visual static. A digital display is inset in a lower corner of the tape. It records the hour and minute, the fleeting seconds and tenths of seconds.

Livia rides her bike, visible in the flickering light.

After the tape has run for five or six seconds, there is an interval of agitation caused either by an unsteady camera or some larger disturbance.

The sound throughout is intense and electronic, a synthesized roaring wind.

Slowly the man raises his head toward the camera. The shaking becomes more pronounced and the tape abruptly ends.

The projection lasts fifteen seconds. Livia is briefly visible as the tape runs out. Then darkness.

Scene 2

When the lights come up, Michael Majeski is seated stage right with a male Interviewer. They are situated in the only lighted part of the set, two chairs and a table, and this segment of space represents a corner of Michael's office downtown.

An elaborate audio-taping device sits on the table between the men. It glows throughout the interview.

INTERVIEWER
What?

MICHAEL
I didn't say anything.

INTERVIEWER
I said something. I said what. What happened next?

MICHAEL
What happened next. It's hard to say.

INTERVIEWER
But once you realized. You must have felt.

MICHAEL
What?

14

INTERVIEWER

I don't know.

MICHAEL

Out of place, I guess. Displaced or misplaced. Somewhere else.

INTERVIEWER

But you *were* somewhere else. This is the point.

MICHAEL

I don't mean in body only. Somewhere else in a deeper way. Somebody somewhere else. I'm trying to be completely clear.

INTERVIEWER

Just keep talking.

MICHAEL

It was one big enormous stupefying shock.

INTERVIEWER

The tape is running.

MICHAEL

I felt remote. I felt a tremendous separation.

INTERVIEWER

From what?

MICHAEL

From what. From everything. Physically safe. Physically fine. But cut off from everything around me. And from myself as well.

INTERVIEWER

As if what?

MICHAEL

Some stranger had crept inside, like surreptitiously, to eat my air-line food. Or someone had been superimposed on me, a person with my outline and shoe size but slyly and fundamentally different. I didn't know how to react. I thought, What is going on?

INTERVIEWER

Where am I?

MICHAEL

Who am I?

INTERVIEWER

How did I get here?

MICHAEL

Where am I going?

INTERVIEWER

And was there any point in the unfolding of this event when you began to see the whole thing as hugely and vastly comic?

MICHAEL

Certainly not in the early and middle stages.

INTERVIEWER

But once you realized.

MICHAEL

Once I realized and spoke to the steward and saw him speak to a flight attendant and saw how word was beginning to spread through the cabin.

INTERVIEWER

Talk faster.

MICHAEL

And realized a word-of-mouth traffic was beginning to build, with amused remarks and maybe some outright laughter and many glances—many, many glances in my direction.

INTERVIEWER

Tell us everything.

MICHAEL

People a little embarrassed on my behalf but also sympathetic and amused and delighted as the story spread. People came to my seat and asked questions. I explained to people what had probably gone wrong, step by step, as best I could reconstruct. Do you want me to reconstruct?

INTERVIEWER

There isn't time.

MICHAEL

Word spread through the cabin in two languages. A telling and retelling of all the little accidents, of all the misunderstandings and mishaps. The whole daylong series. The strangeness.

INTERVIEWER

What strangeness?

MICHAEL

The strangeness. The whole progression. The succession of strange and random things. The whole long sequence of interlocking events that had to happen precisely as they happened before I could make the enormous mistake I made.

INTERVIEWER

I think that does it.

Interviewer turns off the tape machine. The glow begins to fade.

MICHAEL
What?

INTERVIEWER
I think that does it.

MICHAEL
If you want me to clarify or expand upon.

INTERVIEWER
I think that does it. When we air, I'll do a fill-in. Some editing.
Some ambient noise.

MICHAEL
Or if any additional questions come to mind.

INTERVIEWER
I think that does it. I got everything I need.

MICHAEL
I'll give you some numbers you can call. Home. I have home. I
have here. I have my private number for here. I have my secre-
tary when I'm away.

INTERVIEWER
I got everything I need. Just tell me what's your name again.

Scene 3

The living room. Livia rides her exercise bike, facing upstage, her eyes on the TV set that's located in a media cabinet on the back wall. She is looking at Michael's head, which fills the screen, his lips moving soundlessly.

In time, Livia reaches for the remote control unit that's velcro'd to her ankle like an off-duty gun.

She aims the remote and hits the sound button.

The ensuing voices belong to Michael and a female Interviewer.

INTERVIEWER
But first you left the terminal, you boarded the aircraft. Then what?

MICHAEL
Then what. We took off. We flew.

INTERVIEWER
And you reached cruising altitude. And you leveled off. And you ate the snack they gave you. Tell us. Speak. And no lingering suspicion that something was wrong.

MICHAEL
Only the sense of leaving earth. This always seems slightly disallowable.

INTERVIEWER

But you were convinced in your own mind that nothing was realistically amiss. You were snug in your seat and secure in your sense of destination.

MICHAEL

We took off. We flew. I was more or less.

INTERVIEWER

Systems heaving and breathing all around you. Tell us. That sort of essence in the air. That sort of underbreath of powerful thrilling systems.

Lights down on living room.

Lights up on interview space, stage left. Michael seated in chair. Interviewer down on one knee before him and to his left. Camera is inferred, near the stage apron. Interviewer is out of camera range and holds a clipboard, which she consults occasionally as Michael speaks. A glowing mike is fixed to a boom that juts from the wings.

MICHAEL

I was substituting for a colleague in the hospital. I'd never done this trip before.

INTERVIEWER

But first let's take our viewers back to the beginning. Coffee's on the stove.

MICHAEL

Newspaper's on the table.

INTERVIEWER

Radio's buzzing with world events. Where is wife Livia at this point?

20

MICHAEL

She's in the living room on her exercise bike, watching TV.

INTERVIEWER

You are listening to the news and reading the news. She is watching the news.

MICHAEL

We have it covered at every outlet.

INTERVIEWER

Look at the camera, not at me.

MICHAEL

I was substituting for a colleague with a rare disease.

INTERVIEWER

But first you're at the breakfast table staring at your eggs.

MICHAEL

Then I'm out the door, I'm in the taxi, I'm headed to the airport where I intend to catch my flight to what I *think* will be Chicago. They'll meet me in Chicago, a car and driver, and we'll proceed to Valparaiso.

INTERVIEWER

Is that how it's pronounced?

MICHAEL

Indiana. A distance of forty measly miles. I don't know how it's pronounced. I'd never done this trip before. He had an unnamed rare disease.

INTERVIEWER

But first let's go back to the moment you opened your eyes.

MICHAEL
I opened my eyes in the predawn dark.

INTERVIEWER
Tell us precisely what you did.

MICHAEL
I remember reaching sort of drowsy across the bed. Where Livia was lying sprawled.

INTERVIEWER
Use the present tense, please.

MICHAEL
She is downy and dreamy and rumpled.

INTERVIEWER
In pajamas perhaps? An old-fashioned nightie? We need to know. An extra-long T-shirt? What's printed on the shirt? Tell us precisely what you saw. Or nude in raveled sheets, responding only slowly to your touch. Tell us everything. Or restless and stirring. That sort of underbreath of stale sleep and bedsheets and body heat.

MICHAEL
She's warm and soft.

INTERVIEWER
And you're warm and hard.

Lights down on interview space.

Light up on living room. Livia watches TV, pedaling faster or slower depending on the cadence of the voices.

MICHAEL

Barely looking at each other because it's too early in the morning to look. Does she even know who I am? Warm woozy kisses—kisses from the depths of sleep, undefined and musty. But not too many. Practically none. None in fact. Not one skimpy kiss. We aren't here to kiss.

INTERVIEWER

It's predawn. It's present tense.

MICHAEL

Her body heaving and breathing. Hand guiding and sliding. Does she even know it's me? Does she remotely care?

INTERVIEWER

It's sex without personal histories. It's sex stripped of culture.

MICHAEL

The moment does not whisper the usual things.

INTERVIEWER

There's no rustle of slidy nylon. Or breath of velvet innuendo. It's speechless. It's sleepy.

MICHAEL

It's all the things that begin with the letter s.

INTERVIEWER

But not completely subhuman. Not some furry coupling designed to reproduce the beaver species so they can fell their trees and build their beaver dams to whatever mysterious ecological end and deep personal satisfaction.

MICHAEL

And my lovely vivid Livia. Placing her webless hand. Palming my living thing.

INTERVIEWER
It's the dark part of the morning.

Lights down on living room.

Lights up on interview space.

MICHAEL
Does she even open her eyes to see that it's me?

INTERVIEWER
But first let's go back to the night before. You're pouring a drink for yourself and thinking about the trip. Everything seems absolutely normal. Speak. Tell us, Michael. We deeply need to know.

Scene 4

The living room, minus the bike. Michael and a male Interviewer sit on the sofa. They both lean toward the compact tape recorder on the coffee table. The Interviewer is fiddling with the instrument.

MICHAEL
So the magazine will run this, you think, in what?

INTERVIEWER
Two weeks tops. We have a short lead time.

MICHAEL
So when we start the interview.

INTERVIEWER
This is the interview.

MICHAEL
I mean when we formally start. On the record.

INTERVIEWER
This is on the record. Everything is on the record. Everything is the interview.

MICHAEL
So you're saying—what? The interview is already underway?

The interview was underway when I pulled into your driveway. It was underway when I put the key in the ignition in my own driveway. It was underway when you got on the wrong plane and went to the wrong place. The interview started before that. How far back do you want to go? The interview started basically when your father fucked your mother on a rainy night in May.

Pause.

MICHAEL
I accept that. I understand the need for that.

INTERVIEWER
You've done how many of these?

MICHAEL
I have a diary. I've started a journal with all the particulars. I'm into double figures.

INTERVIEWER
Good. I'm going to ask you the same questions everyone else has asked you.

MICHAEL
But you want me to frame my replies somewhat differently. I understand that.

INTERVIEWER
No, you don't.

MICHAEL
You don't want the exact same words I've used before.

INTERVIEWER
Yes, I do.

MICHAEL
You want me to respond exactly.

INTERVIEWER
Frame the same replies.

Pause.

MICHAEL
I can do that. I think that's completely doable.

The Interviewer finishes his adjustments and repositions the tape recorder in the middle of the table. Both men lean close. The instrument begins to glow.

INTERVIEWER
Say something.

MICHAEL
I was substituting for a colleague with a rare disease. And I was standing at the podium in the boarding area preparatory to boarding my flight to Chicago. Passenger X, please present yourself at the podium. What I *think* will be Chicago. They'll meet me in Chicago, a car and driver, and we'll proceed to Valparaiso. However it's pronounced. Indiana. A distance of forty measly miles.

INTERVIEWER
A little faster.

MICHAEL
But the ticket woman at the podium happens to glance at my itinerary. The ticket is fine. The flight to Chicago is entered correctly.

INTERVIEWER
Do I need to hear this in real time?

MICHAEL
It happened in real time.

INTERVIEWER
Give me faster.

MICHAEL
She says, "Why are you going to Chicago if your itinerary says Miami?" And she rustles the sheet of paper my company's travel agent attached to the ticket.

INTERVIEWER
What does the paper say?

MICHAEL
That I don't want to go to Valparaiso, Indiana. That I want to go to Valparaiso, Florida.

INTERVIEWER
Good. That's great. Go on.

Livia enters with fruit juice and sandwiches on a tray. She places the tray on the coffee table and sits in a chair nearby.

MICHAEL
I'm standing there shocked. I'd never done this trip before. He had a virus they could not identify. I didn't know the account. I'd grabbed the briefing papers, grabbed the ticket folder and gone out the door. I knew what the ticket said. But I hadn't read the itinerary. I was only filling in.

INTERVIEWER
Why didn't you call your office from the airport?

MICHAEL

It was too early in the morning. There was no one there. And there was no time for me to call Information and locate the client in whichever Valparaiso.

LIVIA

That's such a beautiful name. That's a stunningly beautiful name.

MICHAEL

Valparaiso is quite beautiful, yes. And Indiana in its own right.

LIVIA

Yes, together they are truly and actually stunning. I'm thinking, Horse farms and rolling hills. A beautiful place to raise children.

INTERVIEWER

Do you have children?

LIVIA

I'm thinking, Deep, still, summer afternoons. Picnics in the high meadows. We have a school-age son. He lives with his grandparents.

INTERVIEWER

Why doesn't he live here, with his parents?

MICHAEL

It's temporary.

LIVIA

He'll be back. You're not eating my sandwiches.

INTERVIEWER

What do you do when your husband's gone?

LIVIA

I ride my bike. I do demon repetitions on my bike. I have a demonic side that only Michael knows.

INTERVIEWER

How does this demonic side show itself?

LIVIA

By making frantic sandwiches. By hurling itself full-length into the world. I feel things. I become addicted to things. Life is habit-forming. I start things and can't stop. I'm dangerous to myself. Michael is dangerous to others.

INTERVIEWER

Should I ask you what you mean by that?

LIVIA

Ask anything. I'll tell you anything. I've found new levels of openness since Michael made his breathtaking journey.

INTERVIEWER

And how did you find out what had become of your husband when that long day and that long journey finally ended?

LIVIA

I found out on the telephone, when he called me, early the next morning, on my stationary bike, and I laughed and laughed.

INTERVIEWER

In relief.

LIVIA

In relief, in wonder. I laughed in wonder. I laughed in astonishment. I could not stop laughing.

MICHAEL
They called me Miguel.

INTERVIEWER
Where, in Miami?

MICHAEL
No, in Santiago.

INTERVIEWER
But first you had to make the Miami mistake.

LIVIA
She says, "Why are you going to Chicago if your itinerary says Miami?"

MICHAEL
I'm shocked senseless and breathless. Is the ticket wrong or is the itinerary wrong? I have no time to find out. She tries to be helpful. There's a Miami flight she can hold if I start running for the gate in about half a second. Or I can board right here for Chicago in a relaxed and civilized manner.

INTERVIEWER
Give me everything that happened.

MICHAEL
She looks at her screen. She sees Miami. She sees an empty seat. But I am leaning toward Chicago.

INTERVIEWER
Give me faster.

MICHAEL
I went to bed the night before *thinking* Chicago. I made love to my wife in the predawn dark in a vague aura of Chicago.

INTERVIEWER
Then what?

MICHAEL
I start to run. Then what. I run. I make up my mind and run. She holds Miami for me and I look at her and run. I run for the gate at the far end of the terminal. I run senselessly and breathlessly.

INTERVIEWER
Faster.

MICHAEL
I run past people with carry-on and people with baggage carts and I run past shuttle buggies filled with people and carry-on and bulging baggage and interracial babies.

LIVIA
Someone, please, eat my sandwiches.

MICHAEL
Anonymous people hurrying toward their lives.

Interviewer takes a sandwich.

INTERVIEWER
Then what?

MICHAEL
I'm watching the takeoff on live video. I'm on the plane, I'm in my seat. There's a monitor on the bulkhead. I look at the monitor and the plane is taking off. I look out the window and the plane is taking off. Then what. The plane is taking off outside the cabin and the plane is taking off inside the cabin. I look at the monitor, I look at the earth.

INTERVIEWER
Then what?

MICHAEL
Then what.

INTERVIEWER
Then what?

Scene 5

The living room in semidarkness. Michael sits in a chair, crouched and waiting. He is drinking a scotch on the rocks. The telephone is in front of him, on the coffee table, and he watches it and waits, breathing audibly.

When the phone rings, he picks it up at once.

MICHAEL

Yes. This is Michael Majeski. Hello, ABC Australia. Yes. I understand we are speaking live. What time is it there? No. What time is it there? Yes. I'm learning Spanish on tape. Yes. Some stranger had crept inside, like surreptitiously, to eat my airline food. No. The moment does not whisper the usual things. No. She brushes her teeth with baking soda. Yes. When I saw the towering mountains capped with snow. That's when I realized. Yes. That's when I realized. No. It was hugely and vastly comic. He had an unnamed rare disease. Pick up the white courtesy phone, please. Yes. But first I'm at the breakfast table staring at my eggs. No. What day is it there? No. What day is it there? Yes. When I saw the towering mountains capped with snow. That's when I realized there was something terribly, terribly wrong. No. She jerked me off in a taxi once. Yes. I was treated wonderfully, wonderfully well. They called me Miguel.

Scene 6

The living room. Livia enters followed by a male Filmmaker/Interviewer and a three-person Camera Crew. Lights. A hand-held camera. Sound equipment. The three people are yoked to each other by a series of wires and cables.

The exercise bike sits in the room.

Livia wears a Day-Glo clip-on mike.

LIVIA
I think we ought to do it outside, by the big maple. It speaks of peace and rest, home at last.

INTERVIEWER
Whatever's shootable. That's what we shoot.

LIVIA
He could sit in a lounging chair with the Sunday papers strewn about.

INTERVIEWER
He could gesture with his glasses, if he wears glasses. We don't give a damn. The man's finally home. Ready to reflect a bit.

LIVIA
He's home and he's exhausted. Sixty-seven interviews in four

and a half days in three and a half cities. I don't think he's capable of saying one more word until he's had a few hours' sleep.

The Crew follows Livia through the scene, filming and recording. They break off once or twice to film the Interviewer and then each other.

INTERVIEWER
I've seen him on daytime and I've heard him on drive-time and we want to do serious work but only if he submits to the idea.

LIVIA
What's the idea?

INTERVIEWER
A feature-length documentary film. A self-commenting super-vérité in which everything that goes into the making of the film *is* the film. Everything that leads up to the film and flows out of the film *is* the film. Including the film. A film that consumes itself even as the audience watches.

LIVIA
But with a central element.

INTERVIEWER
Michael Majeski. A film that wonders which is the true journey. The long flight he made to the bottom of the world. Or what he's experienced since he returned.

LIVIA
The long-range plan?

INTERVIEWER
We record every syllable. Shoot every pore in his body. We shoot his interviews. We follow him to airports, hotels, public toilets.

We get the byplay in the jetway. Because this is the subject. This is the object. We take every stray moment and follow it to the last dripping shiver. Because it's more, it's less, it's better, it's faster, it's true.

LIVIA
And the immediate plan?

INTERVIEWER
We want to shoot some footage while he sleeps.

LIVIA
But won't he mind?

INTERVIEWER
He won't know.

LIVIA
But he'll know when he wakes up.

INTERVIEWER
We won't tell him.

LIVIA
But he'll know when he sees the film.

INTERVIEWER
Tough luck. Too late.

LIVIA
But there's something tender about sleep. It's so totally unprotected.

INTERVIEWER
It's what he wants. It's what brings him into being.

LIVIA

Sleep?

INTERVIEWER

Film. We film mass suicides on raging freeways. What's a sleeping man?

LIVIA

All right. What do we do when he wakes up?

INTERVIEWER

It's all footage waiting to be shot. This man in particular. This man's a modern phenomenon. A business traveler who blundered into a kind of epic adventure. And now he's home for a couple of days.

LIVIA

Ready to reflect a bit.

INTERVIEWER

I've shot reflective interviews with famous felons. White-collar criminals of flawless bearing. It goes like this. He does his prison time. He grows his beard. He writes his book. He learns how to gesture with his glasses. And then he spends the rest of his life in his book-lined study. Doing guilt-ridden interviews with anyone who asks.

LIVIA

But Michael hasn't committed a crime. Michael isn't guilty.

Pause.

INTERVIEWER

Where's your son's room?

LIVIA
Next to ours.

INTERVIEWER
The boy's empty room. I'll want to shoot some footage.

LIVIA
All right. But why?

INTERVIEWER
Because here it is. Because look at it. What a bare and haunted space. I'd frankly like to film you on your bike. And maybe we can talk at some point about your larger ongoing role in this documentary.

LIVIA
It sounds deeply possible.

INTERVIEWER
Downtown.

LIVIA
First thing.

INTERVIEWER
Next week.

LIVIA
Let's.

INTERVIEWER
Do.

LIVIA
Lunch.

Scene 7

The living room. A female Interviewer is seated cross-legged on the floor. She has a notebook and a Day-Glo ballpoint pen and she is waiting. Michael enters speaking. Interviewer begins to write. She takes notes on and off through the scene.

MICHAEL
They called three times today. They're such sad, decent, tired, middle-minded people. I told them. I said I couldn't do it anymore. There are just so many hours in the day. I need some space for a change. Some time to unwind. Too many commitments. Too much nerve-racking travel.

INTERVIEWER
And this means.

MICHAEL
Yes.

INTERVIEWER
You're turning down all further requests for interviews.

MICHAEL
No. I'm quitting my job. I'm giving up my job. They're such docile, dreary, pockmarked people. Do you want me to talk fast, slow—whatever.

INTERVIEWER
I want you to tell me about the moment in the flight when you
begin to realize.

MICHAEL
I'm well into the flight before I begin to realize.

INTERVIEWER
My God. What?

MICHAEL
I have no idea how to get from Miami, Florida to Valparaiso,
Florida.

INTERVIEWER
You're thinking, Where is this place?

MICHAEL
I have no idea.

INTERVIEWER
Is it a suburb of Miami?

MICHAEL
I don't know.

INTERVIEWER
Shall I move about the cabin and ask?

MICHAEL
This is exactly what I do.

INTERVIEWER
Maybe one of the passengers can tell me.

MICHAEL

But no one's heard of Valparaiso, Florida. They've heard of Valparaiso, Indiana.

INTERVIEWER

That's such a beautiful name.

MICHAEL

And Indiana in its own right.

INTERVIEWER

And Florida in its own right.

MICHAEL

Where are you from?

INTERVIEWER

Can you guess?

MICHAEL

Let me see if I can guess.

INTERVIEWER

People are always trying to guess.

MICHAEL

I don't think I can.

INTERVIEWER

They never can.

MICHAEL

But you're here permanently now.

INTERVIEWER

Who knows? Who cares?

MICHAEL
Are you involved with someone?

INTERVIEWER
I don't like that word.

MICHAEL
Are you having a relationship?

INTERVIEWER
I hate that word. Please. I hate all the words in that sentence. And I feel terribly vulnerable—another word I hate—when I find myself in a stranger's home saying these intimate things.

MICHAEL
You haven't said anything.

INTERVIEWER
What should I say? That my life is so unsingular I barely know myself in a mirror.

MICHAEL
This is how I used to feel.

INTERVIEWER
What should I say? That the term itself—my life—is a desperate overstatement.

MICHAEL
This is how I used to feel.

INTERVIEWER
Then you know. How some people are able to use that term and make it sound like a throbbing corporate enterprise.

MICHAEL
Stock options.

INTERVIEWER
Severance packages.

MICHAEL
I used to envy that.

INTERVIEWER
Then you know. How some people manage to live so dynami-
cally. It's a mystery to me how this happens. I interview people
all the time. A man walks in the room, so powerful and smooth.
Like poured concrete. My experience seems puny next to his. Or
women with hair and nails. They look right through me. They
don't catch my name. They don't really hear my questions.
Women in storm-trooper underwear. They open their mouths
and stuff comes out.

She is taking notes, intermittently, as she speaks.

MICHAEL
And you write it down.

INTERVIEWER
And people remarkably read it.

MICHAEL
What kind of underwear?

INTERVIEWER
Women in black strappy underwear. I can sense it under their
clothes. Self-assertive.

MICHAEL
What else?

INTERVIEWER
Executive-sexy. They open their mouths.

MICHAEL
And the men. What?

INTERVIEWER
Stuff comes out.

MICHAEL
A man and woman in a walled space.

INTERVIEWER
He sits there so real. And I wonder what I look like to him. And what would happen if I stop asking questions and he stops answering. Because it's all implied, isn't it?

MICHAEL
In the sense that major things are implied in minor moments.

INTERVIEWER
In the sense that personal things.

MICHAEL
In impersonal moments.

INTERVIEWER
And I wonder what he's thinking in his male-type mind. And what would happen if we stop talking.

They stop talking.

MICHAEL
Then what?

INTERVIEWER

I begin to recognize the moment for what it is. I see the first faint sign of indifference in his eyes. Interview eyes. Soulless, shifting. Tell me this. Why do we keep repeating our failures?

MICHAEL

This is what I used to do.

INTERVIEWER

Then you know. The tiny white sadness of walking out the door. The moonlight wobbling on the river. I get unsettled and confused.

MICHAEL

So do I. Finally someone tells me that Valparaiso is way up in the panhandle part of Florida. Just above the Gulf.

INTERVIEWER

Which means you have to catch another plane.

MICHAEL

And eight and a half hours later.

INTERVIEWER

When this other plane begins its descent. But first. Can I ask you? For my own information.

MICHAEL

Ask anything. Write anything. My wife burned me with a plastic cigarette.

INTERVIEWER

I won't write that.

MICHAEL

She claims to be dangerous only to herself. Then she burns me with a cigarette. She smokes plastic cigarettes. She smokes herbal cigarettes. She gets addicted to whatever's in her mouth.

INTERVIEWER

I thought they were strictly pacifiers. Plastic cigarettes. To chew or suck.

MICHAEL

First she lights them up. Then she sucks them.

INTERVIEWER

Is that what you were arguing about when she burned you? Smoking cigarettes?

MICHAEL

Chewing gum. She chews nicotine gum. More or less incessantly. I told her. I said read the label.

INTERVIEWER

Read the label, please, Livia.

MICHAEL

This product contains nicotine, which may cause fetal harm when administered to a pregnant woman.

INTERVIEWER

I have to ask. Forgive me. Is she pregnant?

MICHAEL

She won't tell me.

INTERVIEWER

Livia, please, I need to know.

MICHAEL

It's one of the things that women hold over men.

INTERVIEWER

Do you want me to stop taking notes?

MICHAEL

Take notes. Take photographs. It's one of the things that women hold and withhold. It's one of your ten thousand uterine secrets. Have you interviewed my wife?

INTERVIEWER

No.

MICHAEL

Interview her uterus. That's where all the plots intersect. Talk to her nipples. Her nipples are sensitive to messages from orbiting satellites. You'll get some stimulating quotes. Talk to her clitoris. You'll have to submit questions in advance. The clitoris doesn't always speak to me. But it will speak to you. It speaks in codes. It speaks in tongues.

INTERVIEWER

I think this is outside the range of my assignment.

MICHAEL

The range is immense and stirring. We took off. We flew.

INTERVIEWER

And eight and a half hours later.

MICHAEL

We came down out of the sky with the seasons reversed.

INTERVIEWER

In Valparaiso, Chile.

MICHAEL

In Santiago, Chile. They put me on a helicopter to Valparaiso. A seaport. Founded 1536. I'm learning Spanish on tape.

INTERVIEWER

But first. Journalistically. After you landed in Miami. And *thought* you were going to Valparaiso, Florida. How did you manage to get on an international flight, even mistakenly, without a passport?

MICHAEL

I had a passport. I had a passport.

INTERVIEWER

Forgive me. But why did you have a passport if you left your house in the morning *thinking* you were going to Valparaiso, Indiana.

MICHAEL

For identification. Airport security. Picture ID.

INTERVIEWER

What about your driver's license?

MICHAEL

I don't have a driver's license. They took it away.

INTERVIEWER

I don't want to know why.

MICHAEL

I'll tell you why.

INTERVIEWER

I've come into a stranger's home to do the most superficial sort of dimwit interview. This is the nature of my assignment.

MICHAEL

I sat behind the wheel, of an automobile, with my blood alcohol level double the legal limit. A state that right-minded drivers, if they want to be survivors—da-da da-da da-da.

INTERVIEWER

I am not writing this.

MICHAEL

But now I'm down out of the sky, in the present tense, with the seasons reversed. They filmed me while I slept.

INTERVIEWER

Didn't you mind?

MICHAEL

I woke up enormously refreshed.

INTERVIEWER

What did you do for a living please? Before you stopped.

MICHAEL

I was an analyst. The company analyzes other companies. At times whole industries. At times whole societies. I analyzed relationships. No, not Philip and Melissa. Or Trish and Todd. Corporate entities. Deep mean massive structures. Are you writing this down?

INTERVIEWER

But first. Can I ask you? For my own human interest.

MICHAEL

How my life.

INTERVIEWER

Yes.

MICHAEL
Has taken on a luminous quality.

INTERVIEWER
Yes.

MICHAEL
A clarity and music. How I see the precise whiteness of the piece of paper you've been writing on. The egg-whitely nuance. The milky nipply nuance. How I see your hand in its particular tonal glow.

INTERVIEWER
What color?

MICHAEL
Flesh color.

INTERVIEWER
My God. What else?

MICHAEL
How swingingly my dick comports itself in and out of my pants. What else. How this and how that. How here and how there. How pain is sharper but death more distant. How death maintains an incandescent distance. Ever since it occurred to me, flying over the snowy mountains, that I was not in Florida anymore.

INTERVIEWER
Please do not move about the cabin when the seatbelt sign is on.

MICHAEL
Place the mask over your nose and mouth.

INTERVIEWER
Please return your food trays to their upright positions.

MICHAEL
What kind of underwear?

INTERVIEWER
Erotomaniacal. Are you a happy man?

MICHAEL
I'm a complete man. How pain is sharper and more primal. How it feels like the first pain ever felt. It has a painness. Do you know what I mean by that? A feltness. And it's far more piercing than anything I've felt before. When she burned me with the cigarette.

INTERVIEWER
Livia, hey, that hurts.

MICHAEL
I felt connected to other people's pain. To pain in other centuries. Pain in literature. To spearheads and smoking swords. Touch me and I flame.

Scene 8

An interview space, center stage. Michael sits at a table equipped with an upright mike. He wears a headset. A control booth is inferred, beyond the stage apron. The male Interviewer's voice floats down from some uncertain point in the building.

INTERVIEWER
Good morning.

MICHAEL
Good morning.

INTERVIEWER
It isn't morning here.

MICHAEL
What is it?

INTERVIEWER
Predawn. Cold and dark. Ever do a remote hookup?

MICHAEL
No. What do I do?

INTERVIEWER
It's simple. I ask questions, you answer. But first. Look

through the panel at the engineer. Wait for him to cue you. Then begin speaking.

                    MICHAEL
What do I say?

                    INTERVIEWER
Anything at all. The engineer has to get a voice level. Speak into the mike.

                    MICHAEL
I see the engineer. Where are you?

                    INTERVIEWER
My body is in Seattle. My voice is in downtown Detroit.

                    MICHAEL
He's cuing me now.

                    INTERVIEWER
Speak in a natural voice. Say anything at all. It's just a test. He needs to find a level.

                    MICHAEL
All right. She doesn't look at me. She says, "Why are you going to Chicago if your itinerary says Miami?" So I don't know whether it's the ticket or the itinerary that's wrong. The ticket has more authority. It's computer processed. It's magnetically printed and coded. The itinerary is a simple piece of paper typed by an ordinary human being. But it doesn't seem gracious to reject Miami only seconds after she has called it up on her screen. She has her keyboard and her screen. She has found a seat for me. I don't want to disappoint her.

                    INTERVIEWER
Wait, wait, wait, wait. The engineer can't find a level. We need

you to be natural and we need you to be interesting. Say something interesting. Speak into the mike. Use your own voice. Be yourself. Be interesting. Keep talking. You have to keep talking.

MICHAEL

All right. She doesn't look at me. They never look at us. How can they? There are long lines of people all the time. She has her console and her random access memory. I have my nitwit piece of paper. But I want something to pass between us. Some nuance of human sharing. Some milky nipply nuance. I look at her face for a sign. A gesture that might echo through our day. But the moment does not whisper the usual things. He had a virus they could not identify.

INTERVIEWER

Wait, wait, wait. Don't be so obsessed. You sound obsessed. Tell you what. Try talking about something else. Change the subject. Relax. We need you to be funny and charming.

MICHAEL

I can do that.

INTERVIEWER

Then do it.

MICHAEL

All right. I'm starting my day. Coffee's on the stove. Newspaper's on the table. Radio's buzzing with world events. Where is wife Livia at this point? Livia's in the living room on her exercise bike, doing demon repetitions. She is smoking her third herbal cigarette of the morning. She chain-smokes herbs and spices. It's the morning after the night. Her eyes are pouchy. Face is drained. This makes me feel some unaccountable guilt. I pour a cup of coffee and take it in to her. I don't know what to say. I can't find a way into some ordinary warmth. Something easy and agreeable.

And I drink, which doesn't help. It helps but doesn't. Does this make sense? Because I've kept on drinking even after the car crash. Because I've kept on drinking because of the car crash. Because she drinks because I drink. I had a passport. I had a passport. But what am I saying when I say this? What's in our lives together, hers and mine, that I can speak about? Do you understand how tremendously dense? A minute in a room, together. How every minute is a recapitulation of her life, or mine. I feel this in a room sometimes. Or both our lives, crowding down on us. Do you see how every half second. Does this make sense? How it squirms with our histories, our psychologies. Do you understand how this agglomeration. I don't know if that's the word. How the simplest exchange. How the smallest half second is so filled and mingled with human miscellany. Nothing can be isolated and identified. There are no facts in a marriage. Do I want to be alone? Terrifies me. But have I learned how to live with someone else? When I saw the towering mountains capped with snow. Who in the pits of existence is she that I have to share with her my every breath? Eyes are pouchy. Face is drained. We'd had an interlude of sex in the predawn dark. Not one skimpy kiss. We aren't here to kiss. Does she even know it's me? Does she remotely care? Does she even open her eyes to see that it's me?

Lights up on living room. Livia rides her bike, facing downstage. She is being filmed by the Camera Crew—lights, sound, handheld camera. She holds a coffee mug while she pedals. She has a Walkman strapped to her upper arm and wears earphones wired to the Walkman.

One thing I'll say. Livia tells the truth about things. She's completely unafraid and I have no choice but to match her. Truth for truth. Lie for lie. She's a virtuoso liar. Nights are vintage misery. We find argument nearly everywhere. It seeps from the walls and comes on with the light in the fridge. Mornings lie thick and still.

In the living room, the three-member Crew moves in for a tight shot, yoked together, crouched low before the stationary bike. Livia pedals, drinking coffee and listening to the radio.

Bringing coffee to my wife on a routine Tuesday in the world. I love her deeply. I love her in the sorest way, in the deepest aching grain of my body, and there are times when I can't bear to look at her or hear the sound of her voice and I'm appalled at my failure to be generous. We've had five specialists look at our son. All their names begin with the letter *F*. It's the untalkative morning. It's the deaf-mute morning after the bang-bang night. I finish my coffee and put on my jacket. She doesn't look at me. They never look at us. How can they? There are long lines of people all the time. She has her keyboard and her screen. She says, "Why are you going to Chicago if your itinerary says Miami?"

Lights down on living room.

The microphone on Michael's table begins to glow.

INTERVIEWER

(*softly*) Four three two one. (*Then booming.*) Sunrise radio. Rise and shine. We're about to speak live with Michael Majeski, who has a humorous story to tell about a long, wrong journey he took after setting out from his home on an ordinary business trip. Let's take our listeners back to the beginning. Michael. You're still in bed, in the predawn dark, and you're waking from a restless sleep. You reach for the bedside light.

Michael makes a half gesture, reaching for an imaginary light. He pauses in midmotion.

BLACK

Act Two

The studio set of a TV talk show. It is a living room set that bears some resemblance to the Majeski living room of Act One.

Cameras, lights and technical personnel are left to the imagination of the audience.

The set is dimly lighted.

Teddy Hodell, the show's announcer and secondary figure, walks out of the wings and takes up a position just outside the set, on the stage apron, from which point he addresses the audience.

TEDDY

Please don't applaud. This is only the warmup. People want to applaud the merest glimpse of me. I understand. They want to applaud my watchband, my bridgework. They want to follow me to the men's room and watch me position myself in a martial stance at the urinal, shoulders squared. I am the first to understand. They want to lift their babies to my gaze. But this is only the warmup. Save your energies and passions for Delfina and her guests. Not that the warmup isn't part of the show. The warmup is taped and studied. The warmup is completely crucial to the furtherance of our endeavor. Take my words to heart. I am here to declare your specialness. I am here to separate you from the grim business of your nonaudience lives. I summon you to a hyperlife of laughter and tears and tenderness and rocking socking sensation. Note well. Delfina draws literal life from her audience. If you are uninspiring, she is stripped of emotional moment. If you are benumbed, she grows weary-winged and indistinct. The lady fades into gray vapor. Consider the central meaning of your role. Global millions watching at home but only a teentsy-weentsy studio audience. You are here and now and body-hot. The cameras will swing toward the audience in the course of the show. Not once but many times. Point to yourselves on the giant monitors. I understand the need for this. I encourage this. Wave to yourselves. See yourselves cross that critical divide into some plane of transcendence. But take my words to fervent heart. If you are listless and brittle, you sink a lank blade in the lady's desolate breast. I am here to raise a final caution. Do *not* applaud her entrance. We use canned applause for Delfina's entrance. We adjust the level to her prevailing mood, to her blood sugar and triglycerides. We match the level to the state of national anxiety and the whistle of the wind in lonely coastal zones. Listen now. Wait. What tender footfall comes stealing eerie out of deep shadow? What pipings of high delight sound in the great halls?

Teddy steps into the set, looking directly into one of the inferred cameras.

Lights up bright. Canned applause fills the hall.

Dear friends. Our life-spirit, the shining soul of daytime America. Delfina Treadwell.

Delfina enters carrying a cordless mike.

Teddy settles into an armchair, where he will remain through the act.

Delfina will move freely about the set, standing, sitting, addressing the studio audience, sometimes looking directly into one of the cameras as she speaks.

All four central figures in the act wear TV makeup, the effect being more pronounced in the case of Delfina and Michael.

DELFINA
I am so glad to be here. I woke up this morning.

TEDDY
Feeling.

DELFINA
So totally unmyself.

TEDDY
How is this different from every other morning?

DELFINA
It isn't. Because this is my stark reality. I can't remember who I am.

TEDDY
What do you do?

DELFINA
I talk on the phone. I begin every day on the touch tone. It's like the intravenous feeding of a comatose woman. This is what I need to bring me back. Voices.

TEDDY
But whose? Former husbands?

DELFINA
Financial planners.

TEDDY
Children bearing murderous grudges?

DELFINA
Tax lawyers. Actuaries. People who take their laptops to the toilet with them.

TEDDY
How we pity you.

DELFINA
He mocks me.

TEDDY
Those of us who have to work for a living.

DELFINA
I sit and listen to them. Crisp and clear. Great big barbered network executives. Aftershave in their voices. On the speaker-
phone they sound like God coming through the roof of a
thirteenth-century cathedral.

TEDDY
And you.

DELFINA
Mumbling in my coffee mug. At that hour? I'm at the language
level of the origin of species.

TEDDY
But then.

DELFINA
But then—I come out here.

TEDDY
They're live.

DELFINA
You're so live. You have real lives. This is what I find—I don't
know, what.

TEDDY
I don't know, what.

DELFINA

Three-dimensional. I'm in the thickness of things. I feel the attraction. Feel the pulling power of your lives. I swear I want to throw my body into the seats sometimes. Teddy is my witness. I think of all the stories in this building. They quiver on my skin. What's more dramatic than the struggle to become a man or woman in the world? What's more rife?

TEDDY

I like that word.

DELFINA

With danger and pain. And the endless tensions—I feel that too. Old longings, unbreathable secrets. Whatever's untold that a telling might snatch from putrefaction. Or do we need our secrets to tell us who we are? The thing is. The point is I feel it. A physical sense of your experience. It's like voltage shooting through my hands. Almost taste your muggy breath. All but touch your flesh where it presses and folds. Bent as you are in your seats.

TEDDY

Slightly clammy.

DELFINA

But all the sexier, yes, in your body-hugging briefs. Teddy knows it's true. Each life so dense and rich. And the lives of the guests.

TEDDY

Who are they when they're not here?

DELFINA

This is what we want to find out. We commit our crimes at night. When do we commit our crimes?

TEDDY
We commit our crimes at night and reveal ourselves in the high noon of studio lights.

DELFINA
This is why we have daytime.

TEDDY
To interpret the night.

DELFINA
To pass judgment on the night. And today we have a nice, bright, interesting couple to talk to. Whose names I have completely.

TEDDY
Michael and Livia.

DELFINA
But first this word.

Lights down on set.

Lights up on Chorus, stage right.

The Chorus consists of three people in stylish civilian versions of flight-crew uniforms. The outfits are severe, faintly intimidating, mostly black and not necessarily matching. Members wear harsh dark makeup.

The Chorus exists in a space separate from the stage proceedings, in another dimension—an eerie fluorescence that suggests the hyperreality of a filmed TV commercial potentially viewable in a thousand cities, at twenty-second intervals, day and night, for an indefinite period of time.

The Chorus recites the longer passages in unison. The middle member alone recites the brief italicized segments while the other

two members gesture in the manner of flight attendants miming
safety instructions before takeoff.

CHORUS
Has anyone had access to your baggage
Has anyone had access
Has anyone given you items to carry
Has anyone in the world
Said anything to you at any time
That might conceivably mean
Has anyone had access to your unspoken thoughts
Since you first became aware

MEMBER
Homemade cookies at thirty thousand feet
Snuggy-bear in your beamy seat
That's executive class on Air Reliance

CHORUS
Did you pack your bags yourself
Has anyone had access
In the event of an evacuation
Has anyone ever said to you
In the fullness of fading time
Pull the mask toward you
Ausgang / Sortie / Salida
Then place the mask   Then place the mask

MEMBER
Cappuccino in a foaming cup
Anonymous sex with the armrests up
That's your overnight flight on Air Reliance

CHORUS
Please make your selection from the following menu
Then place the mask over your nose and mouth

For automated flight information
Has anyone had access
Press or say *one*
Has anyone told you confidentially
Was there ever a moment on the foggy tarmac
When you thought that nothing mattered

Lights down on Chorus.

Lights up on set. Michael and Livia are seated on the sofa. Livia is clearly pregnant. She will remain seated throughout the act.

DELFINA
Livia. Who are you?

LIVIA
I'm a physical therapist in a nursing home. And a part-time unpublished poet.

DELFINA
Do you love your husband?

LIVIA
Yes, I do, deeply.

DELFINA
Do you absolutely ache in your heart sometimes, around the middle of the day, without knowing quite why?

LIVIA
Yes, I do, in my compact car, stopped in traffic somewhere, with my life sort of bug-stuck on the windshield.

DELFINA
Do you like to eat bananas that are slightly overripe?

LIVIA

Yes, I do.

DELFINA

A little bit rotten, even?

LIVIA

Yes, I do. They're funky and sexy and make me think that pleasure is somehow connected—to what?

MICHAEL

Perishability.

DELFINA

I sometimes think I'm clinically self-absorbed. A condition that ought to be covered by health insurance. Do you feel that way about yourself?

LIVIA

Yes, I do. Except my short attention span maybe saves me.

DELFINA

But who are you down deep, alone in the dark?

LIVIA

I'm a little bit of everything around me. Who am I. But completely separate at the same time. I'm whoever it is that has my memories. I'm part my mother, my father, my husband, my son. Part my car, my house. My dog if we had a dog. My hometown, a whole lot. But completely someone separate. I used to be a little knock-kneed. My father called me a knock-kneed creature of the earth. That's who I am.

DELFINA

And you are deeply pregnant.

LIVIA
I am so pregnant.

DELFINA
We don't have unborn babies on the show normally.

TEDDY
They're not consumers. They take up space but do not spend.

*Teddy occasionally browses in a magazine he has taken from the
coffee table.*

DELFINA
Michael. I think everyone already knows how you set out one
morning for Valparaiso, Indiana.

MICHAEL
Is that how it's pronounced?

DELFINA
I wasn't going there. You were going there.

MICHAEL
I'd never done this trip before.

DELFINA
But isn't there something—I don't know. A little raggedy-ass.
About going to a place whose name you don't know how to pro-
nounce.

MICHAEL
It's more than one place and the name is pronounced differently, depending.

DELFINA

You pronounce it the same way, everywhere.

MICHAEL

I was substituting for a colleague with a rare disease.

DELFINA

How you set out one morning for Valparaiso, Indiana. And ended up in Valparaiso, Chile. Roughly six thousand miles off the mark. Give or take.

MICHAEL

There's a documentary film in postproduction right now. There's a book deal in the works. My website drew five thousand hits last week. I want to grow a beard.

DELFINA

What else?

MICHAEL

I go on motivational speaking tours. What else. I do autograph shows on weekends.

DELFINA

What do you autograph?

MICHAEL

Plane tickets mostly. People in long shuffling lines. A movie producer has taken an option on my life.

DELFINA

Your life.

MICHAEL

She said, "Why are you going to Chicago if your itinerary says Miami?"

DELFINA

The life of a man who has been talking nonstop about his win-some misadventure. But has he ever approached a moment. People. Of self-recognition.

TEDDY

Self-knowledge.

DELFINA

We want to know if he understands the true nature of his acts. From the heart of the culture.

TEDDY

Into the heart of the man.

DELFINA

You've spoken about your arrest for drunken driving.

MICHAEL

My blood alcohol level was double the legal limit.

LIVIA

Our son was in the car with his father.

DELFINA

Personalize him for us. Please.

LIVIA

Andy. Sitting next to his father in the front seat. Brown-haired. In jeans with plaid lining. Slightly sweaty. After a day of play.

MICHAEL

I did not fasten his seatbelt.

TEDDY

Fasten your seatbelt by inserting the metal end into the buckle.

DELFINA

Unseatbelted. Seriously injured. And psychologically damaged as well. But you know what?

LIVIA

I forgave Michael on the Shopping Network.

TEDDY

We don't want to hear about that.

DELFINA

We're not interested in that. We're interested in the tragic fact that an individual conceals from himself. Michael. What are you hiding in your heart?

MICHAEL

There's nothing I haven't openly spoken about. I've answered every question. I've answered some questions seventy, eighty, ninety times. I've answered in the same words every time. I do the same thoughtful pauses in the exact same places. We're dealing with the important things here. Our faith, our health. Who we are and how we live. And I'm beginning to think that people need my story. There's something in the symmetry of my mistake that shakes the heart and approaches a condition of wonder.

LIVIA

He wants to go back there.

MICHAEL

I'm learning Spanish on tape.

LIVIA

We want a bilingual baby.

MICHAEL

I'm studying maps of South America. I have map fever. There are maps all over the house. I want evidence of my journey. The reality of it. The vast distances on the flat map surface. The map makes the distances real.

LIVIA

The journey was unreal. I found out on the telephone, when he called me, early the next morning, on my stationary bike, and I laughed and laughed.

DELFINA

Teddy.

MICHAEL

It was hugely and vastly comic.

DELFINA

Tell them to shut up.

TEDDY

Be nice. Ask them about their marriage.

DELFINA

That's so unseductive a subject.

TEDDY

We have to peel away the outer layers. Don't you think? One by one.

DELFINA

I hate these unraveling relationships.

TEDDY

You hate that word.

DELFINA

I hate all the words in that sentence.

TEDDY

Because you take them personally. You take everything personally.

DELFINA

The squeezing of spaces. That's what marriage means to me. It's the dark side of the moon of playing house. The littleness of every word and phrase. What else?

MICHAEL

The enforced intimacy.

DELFINA

Who said that? Did someone say something? Michael. There are certain men who make wonderful husbands for second wives. Are you one of these? Is Livia marked for disposal? Do you need the ruin of your first marriage before you can ease into mature contentment with wife number two? Younger of course, and far more compliant, and greatly adept at all kinds of sex.

MICHAEL

Livia is greatly adept at all kinds of sex.

DELFINA

Does she want to talk about that?

LIVIA

I'll talk about anything with you, Delfina, because I feel I know you. Oral, genital.

DELFINA

Do you talk about these things with your husband?

LIVIA

Sex is more intense since Michael made his journey. It's sex with an edge. We do it but don't talk about it.

MICHAEL

We do it without leading into it. We don't draw the curtains or turn down the sheets.

LIVIA

We do it standing or sitting.

MICHAEL

We take our pleasure.

LIVIA

We take our showers.

MICHAEL

We don't talk or moan. There's nothing smooth or rhythmic. It's edgy and impersonal. You ought to try it, Delfina.

LIVIA

We do it standing up. Before I got big. Or he bends me over in a moonlit room.

MICHAEL

We don't draw the curtains. We don't moan or sigh. It's very intense sex. We barely recognize ourselves as being whoever we are.

LIVIA

We used to do it on my bike, America.

MICHAEL

We take our showers.

LIVIA

We go to sleep.

DELFINA

But do you lie awake sometimes and feel the genius and terror of night?

LIVIA

Yes, I do, actually.

DELFINA

What kind of dentifrice do you use and how many times a day?

LIVIA

I brush my teeth with baking soda. I'm addicted to it. I brush and brush. It seeps into the gums and makes me feel immortal.

DELFINA

Is there something you want the whole world to know about Livia Majeski?

LIVIA

I love to wash my pussy after sex. I love the water soothing from the showerhead. My soapy fingers in my crotch. The slobber of the body and the erotic animal fat of the mass-produced soap. The same brand of soap in ten million showers with adjustable showerheads. I love to bathe and shower and smoke and stop smoking. How many times have I stopped smoking?

MICHAEL

She burned me once with a plastic cigarette.

DELFINA

We're not interested in that.

LIVIA

I love to wash my body and dry my body and brush my teeth and baste my turkey. I have orgasms that last all day. I take them to the dry cleaner and the shoe repair.

DELFINA

And you feel you know me. And maybe I feel. What do I feel, Teddy?

TEDDY

You feel what you frequently feel on the show. An insight into the true nature of a person or a situation.

DELFINA

On the show and nowhere else incidentally.

TEDDY

As it should be. The show is your heightened brightened self. Nowhere else is nowhere else.

DELFINA

Livia. This primate fetus you're schlepping around under your belly button. Was it conceived in the traditional sort of in-your-face manner?

LIVIA

Yes, it was.

DELFINA

It did not result.

LIVIA

No.

DELFINA

From an impersonal spurt of fluid. Belonging to some lonely donor. Locked in a bone-cold cubicle.

LIVIA

No.

DELFINA
With his girlie magazine.

TEDDY
And his hard-on in his hand.

DELFINA
Somewhere in the windswept world.

LIVIA
It was not remote. It was not nameless. It was totally knowing the person.

DELFINA
Who was the person? Whose baby is it? Is it Michael's?

Pause.

LIVIA
No, it isn't. Why do you ask?

Michael gets up and walks to the other end of the set, where he stands staring at Livia.

DELFINA
I ask because—why do I ask?

TEDDY
Because why else would she be here?

DELFINA
Why else would you be here? Would you be so flauntingly pregnant if the child were your husband's? What's the point of that? You are here to unfurl your crime across the satellite skies.

81

TEDDY
She is here to shame her spouse and seek redemption.

DELFINA
But we're not running a redemption racket. And we're not interested in why you did it or with whom.

LIVIA
It was a documentary filmmaker. In a cheapo motel.

TEDDY
This is so deeply tabloid tedious.

LIVIA
He looked at me at lunch. There were walnuts in my salad. We
got in his car and went to the room.

DELFINA
This makes me feel ritually unclean.

LIVIA
He doesn't know it's his child. This is a shock to him too.
Whose name I won't mention in case he's watching with family
and friends.

MICHAEL
Thank you for your protective instincts. Mother.

DELFINA
Michael. Do not drift out of camera range. Please.

TEDDY
We commit our crimes at night.

LIVIA

It was hard, bright, brutal daylight. We disrobed each other slowly until we were in matching states of respective undress. I unzipped him with my teeth.

DELFINA

We don't want to know what happened next.

LIVIA

His penis flopped out of his pants. *Boing.* Like a tumbling drunk.

DELFINA

People. This is not the level we aspire to.

LIVIA

I don't want to become a gaunt woman with a shattering secret. He's the father of our child. Michael's and mine.

DELFINA

Do not disappear off camera. Michael. Or none of this will have happened. Off-camera lives are unverifiable.

TEDDY

He'll cause a warp in the information flow.

DELFINA

We'll all wake up tomorrow to find we've never been born. Come. Sit with Delfina.

MICHAEL

How much time do I get to adjust to the news?

TEDDY

It's an hour show. From the heart of the culture.

DELFINA
Into the heart of the man.

TEDDY
But first this word.

Lights down on set.

Lights up on Chorus, stage left.

CHORUS
In preparation for departure
Pull the mask toward you
For domestic reservations, press or say *two*
Then place the mask   Then place the mask
Has anyone had access
Has anyone ever said to you that shadows
Tend to gather in the dying light of day
If the air system in the cabin suddenly

MEMBER
A video screen attached to your seat
Another pacifying baby treat
That's platinum class on Air Reliance

CHORUS
In the event of a water landing
Has anyone had access to your baggage
Has anyone touched you in a tender place
To inflate the vest
Schwimm westen / Gilets de sauvetage /Chalecos salvavidas
Please make your selection from the following menu
In the event of a vertical descent
Press or say   Press or say

MEMBER
An airline flies on marketing themes
Expressed in rhymes with dingdong schemes
In the self-referring skies of Air Reliance

CHORUS
In the event of a drop in cabin pressure
In the unlikely event
Has anyone had access
Jump onto the slide with legs extended
Then place the mask   Then place the mask
Has anyone had access
Has anyone made an approach
Has anyone ever said what you've never said yourself

Lights down on Chorus.

Lights up on set. Michael is seated again but not next to Livia. He moves about freely during the rest of the act.

LIVIA
I ride my bike and look at Michael. I see him complete when he's on TV. It's the realized potential of the man. He's so really deeply there. The bones in his face seem to glow. He becomes an exceptional being.

DELFINA
He glows.

LIVIA
He shines. In his bronzy-orange makeup. He is bronze-bodied. The sheer magnitude of it. The lovely and touching sort of folly that sent him flying not only to the wrong city but the wrong continent. Half a world away from home.

DELFINA
First you made the Miami mistake.

MICHAEL
I make up my mind and run. She holds Miami for me and I look
at her and run. I run for the gate at the far end of the terminal. I
run senselessly and breathlessly.

TEDDY
Pick up the white courtesy phone, please.

DELFINA
And in Miami. Instead of boarding a little commuter plane to
Valparaiso, Florida.

MICHAEL
Yes. It was strange. The aircraft seemed too big, too wide-bodied
for an intrastate flight.

DELFINA
But you said nothing. The attendant came around with pillows
and blankets.

MICHAEL
And I said nothing. I was intimidated by the systems. The enormous sense of power all around me. Heaving and breathing. How
could I impose myself against this force? The electrical systems.
The revving engines. I was substituting for a colleague in the hospital. The sense of life support. The oxygen in the oxygen masks.

TEDDY
Secure your mask before helping others.

MICHAEL
I felt submissive. I had to submit to the systems. They were all-
powerful and all-knowing. If I was sitting in this assigned seat.

Think about it. If the computers and metal detectors and uniformed personnel and bomb-sniffing dogs had allowed me to reach this assigned seat and given me this airline blanket that I could not rip out of its plastic shroud, then I must belong here. That's how I was thinking at the time.

DELFINA
I don't believe you.

MICHAEL
That's how I was thinking at the time.

DELFINA
Do you believe him?

TEDDY
I don't believe him.

DELFINA
I don't believe him either.

MICHAEL
That I tried to rip out of its plastic shroud with my thumbnail.

DELFINA
I don't believe you.

LIVIA
What do you believe?

DELFINA
This is a man so deep in self-estrangement he conceals his own actions from himself.

LIVIA
He made a series of innocent mistakes. Endearing comic screwups.

DELFINA

It may have begun that way. The ticket said one thing, the itinerary said another. But I believe he sensed. He surely knew at some level. Valparaiso, Indiana. That's where his business was. But he went in the other direction. To the deep end of Latin America.

MICHAEL

We landed in Santiago. And they convinced me. Airline officials. To go on to Valparaiso. To make the mistake complete. For the human interest. For the beauty and balance. The formal resolution.

DELFINA

Only it wasn't a mistake.

MICHAEL

I was treated wonderfully, wonderfully well. They called me Miguel. The mayor of Valparaiso. A seaport. Founded 1536. Came out to greet me.

DELFINA

And your escape had found its second level. Its public life.

LIVIA

There was no escape. Escape from what?

DELFINA

In the airports of the world, what do people do when their planes have landed?

TEDDY

They deplane.

DELFINA

They deplane. Anonymous people hurrying toward their lives. And Michael going the other way. Toward what exactly?

TEDDY
Some sad nameless nowhere.

LIVIA
We deny this, live.

DELFINA
He says one thing but hides another in his heart.

TEDDY
What is he hiding in his heart?

DELFINA
Who is he when he's not here?

TEDDY
What was he running away from?

DELFINA
Not the guilt of a damaged child or troubled marriage. Not even
the heaving mediocrity of his life.

TEDDY
Something deeper.

DELFINA
Who he is.

TEDDY
What's deeper than that?

DELFINA
Who he is.

TEDDY
What's deeper than that?

DELFINA

He wanted to live in the sky, lost to his own knowing.

LIVIA

How can you say these things without the slightest knowledge of the man?

DELFINA

Teddy.

TEDDY

It's her show. She can say anything she wants.

DELFINA

Confirm for us. This whole wandering chronicle. Acknowledge the truth of your journey. At some desperate level you surely knew. Which flight number.

TEDDY

Which departure gate.

DELFINA

Which Valparaiso. Reveal yourself. Who are the gods in your head?

LIVIA

Leave him alone. Bitch. Household name.

DELFINA

What fevers of despair sent you running through terminals? Speak. Tell us, Michael. We deeply need to know.

LIVIA

Why do you need to know?

TEDDY

We need to know everything. We need to show everything.

DELFINA
Because everything's accessible.

TEDDY
Because everything's replayable.

DELFINA
I'm live, I'm taped, I'm run, I'm rerun. I'm on all the time, somewhere in the world. I'm on when no one's watching—in a hotel lobby in Rajasthan somewhere. This is touching to me. I'm haunted by the homeless poetry of this. But you have to understand. People. I'm not part of that empty lobby. No. The lobby, the entire hotel, the Indian subcontinent—these things are part of the TV set that displays my image. The world is sucked up inside a little lonely Sony. Tell me. Is this my sleazy ego speaking?

TEDDY
It's only observable fact.

MICHAEL
I've been candid from the first moment and the first microphone.

DELFINA
I don't want your candor. I want your soul in a silver thimble.

MICHAEL
How do you expect to get it? Something so mysterious.

DELFINA
Then call it the self. I want your naked shitmost self.

MICHAEL
Something so unknowable. Unwordable.

DELFINA

We have time and we have words. Teddy.

TEDDY

We have time.

DELFINA

And we have words. Endless melting words. Words spoken expressly to be forgotten.

MICHAEL

I sit in hotel rooms and watch the show. I watch you. I don't forget what you say. I feel I know you, Delfina.

DELFINA

But I don't know you. Not yet.

MICHAEL

I sit and watch between interviews. Between appearances. I sign autographs on weekends. People in long shuffling lines. They have cataracts and tumors. Sad, decent, tired, orange-peeling people. They have lower back pain. I sign their flight coupons. Their laminated safety cards.

TEDDY

Examine the safety card in the seat pocket in front of you.

DELFINA

What do you see when you look in the mirror?

MICHAEL

Somebody somewhere else.

DELFINA

What part of the paper do you read first?

MICHAEL
I don't read the paper. I don't need the paper. Not anymore. The paper is part of the air I breathe.

DELFINA
Do you remember being born?

MICHAEL
Livia remembers being born. I remember dying.

Delfina and Michael look past each other, each speaking into a different camera.

DELFINA
Do you ever feel so desolate you think you can't possibly bear it?

MICHAEL
You think no one has ever been so incomplete.

DELFINA
You think you're trapped in some walkie-talkie daydream. Abandoned to your own agitated voice.

MICHAEL
Stripped of everything around you. No, I never feel that way.

DELFINA
What fevers of despair?

He addresses her directly.

MICHAEL
What recurring dreams?

DELFINA
There are things I take to make me sleep. Too deep to dream.

MICHAEL
What do you take to make you happy?

DELFINA
I take the network limo. Being here. Being live. This is what makes me happy.

MICHAEL
How do you tell the difference between celebrity and desperation?

DELFINA
I have trouble telling differences in general. I wake up in the morning undifferentiated.

MICHAEL
What do you do in your private moments?

DELFINA
These are my private moments. This is the time I set aside in which to be myself. The studio audience restores my life force. The thing I've misplaced during the night. I feel private here. You have to understand. I live in a box in a state of endless replication. I speak to intimate millions. One of me for each of them. It's the only way to have a conversation. I'm like a primitive painted doll.

TEDDY
Undersized but powerful.

DELFINA
Also vulnerable. Fragile in my nonbox person. My vestigial mortal inch. They hit the channel button on their remotes, repeatedly. It all flows together. Time, space, memory. I'm disturbed by this. I'm hurt in a thousand childlike ways. They are changing channels on me. Where do I go, Daddy, when they hit the button?

TEDDY
To the edge of very hell.

DELFINA
But I flow with it. I accept it. Because they come back to me in
the end. I talk to them in their living rooms, kitchens and crap-
pers. It's the only meaningful exchange. I talk to them in their
messy beds that they can't seem to get out of even in midday, in
midlife (*She speaks into camera*) and there's a thumb-smudge
on the TV screen that's driving you crazy but you can't ever,
somehow, sweetheart, get around to cleaning it, and I understand this because I am human within the guidelines of my terminal wealth and fame, and I tell myself that maybe the
Windex is so low in the bottle that when you press the squirter,
nothing fucking happens. (*She looks at Michael.*) And I sometimes wonder what they're thinking as they watch me.

MICHAEL
I have recurring fantasies.

DELFINA
What kind of fantasies? What kind of dentrifice? What is the
secret you aren't telling?

MICHAEL
I sign their flight coupons. Their voided boarding passes. A
woman gave me her passport to sign. She'd seen me on TV.
Which camera am I talking to?

TEDDY
Talk to camera three.

Michael faces into the inferred camera.

MICHAEL

They shuffle down the line. They have cataracts. They have waterfalls. They have recurring rivers and floods. I answer their eager questions. Moon-faced men and women with yearnings of epic dimension. I tell them I brush my teeth with Close-Up.

DELFINA

Because this is what they want to know.

MICHAEL

Because they see me on TV. The way I see you when I'm in my room.

DELFINA

Don't fight the camera. Melt into it.

MICHAEL

The way I see you when I'm in my room.

DELFINA

Do we make eye contact? Eye contact has implications. Look at me. Let me ease you toward a sense of self-enlightenment.

MICHAEL

Explain me to myself.

DELFINA

Bring you gently into clear-heartedness.

MICHAEL

Explain me to myself, you'll make me choke on my lunch. Feel sympathy for me, I'll puke monkey blood on your understated shoes.

DELFINA

Michael. Dear Man. Miguel. There's something you recall so darkly you call it dying.

TEDDY

I remember dying.

DELFINA

Livia remembers being born. You said.

TEDDY

I remember dying.

DELFINA

There's something you experienced on the long flight down the world.

MICHAEL

Why do you need to know?

Delfina caresses him lightly from behind.

DELFINA

Because we can't stop needing. Because everything's disposable.

TEDDY

Because everything's replaceable.

DELFINA

All those signal grids, evenly beating in the night sky. Think what would happen if we didn't fill the grids. People. Pause and think. If the grids break down. Think how empty it would be. Suddenly nothing. Would be dark. Would be bleak. All the words that end in the letter *k*. What is out there? Who are we? Would be infinite winter in our rooms.

MICHAEL

I saw the towering mountains capped with snow. I thought, What is going on?

TEDDY

Where am I?

MICHAEL

Who am I?

TEDDY

How did I get here?

MICHAEL

Where am I going? And I knew there was nowhere else to take my sorry life.

DELFINA

You'd run out of airspace and landscape. You were in a state of personal—what do we want to call it?

TEDDY

What do we want to call it?

DELFINA

Panic. Of many months running.

MICHAEL

Years actually. And I realized I was improvising a journey that had its own stone logic. Meant to end one way only.

DELFINA

Don't fight the camera. Melt into it.

MICHAEL
I took my airline blanket and my shaving kit to the toilet. I took out my razor. I removed the blade from the razor.

DELFINA
What brand?

MICHAEL
What brand. Wilkinson Sword.

DELFINA
Tell us everything.

MICHAEL
Spearheads and smoking swords.

DELFINA
Holding the blade delicately. Double-edged. But determined, yes. Because you'd run out of world in which to live.

MICHAEL
In an airline toilet. With my shitmost self.

DELFINA
Systems heaving and breathing all around you. Tell us. That sort of essence in the air. Prepared to slit one of the major arteries of your body.

MICHAEL
No.

DELFINA
The artery in the neck. Teddy. That carries blood to the head.

From behind, Delfina runs her microphone caressingly over Michael's face and neck.

MICHAEL
No. Prepared to slit the plastic shroud in which the blanket was sealed. Because I could not rip it open with my thumbnail.

DELFINA
Abandoned to your own agitated voice.

MICHAEL
Yes.

DELFINA
Stripped of everything around you.

MICHAEL
Yes.

DELFINA
Tell us. Speak.

MICHAEL
I slit open the plastic shroud. Put the blade back in the razor. The razor back in the kit. I removed the blanket from the shroud and lowered the toilet lid. I placed the folded blanket on the lid.

Teddy mimes these actions in flight-attendant fashion.

DELFINA
Then what?

MICHAEL
I sat on the toilet. Then what. I took my dental floss out of the kit. I placed the plastic shroud over my head and drew it snug

around my neck and fastened the bottom with a long strand of floss, round and round and round, triple tight.

Teddy mimes these actions.

DELFINA
Waxed or unwaxed. Because this is what we need to know.

TEDDY
We need to know everything.

MICHAEL
I began to not be able to breathe. Time passed, uneventfully. I began to work out my dying.

DELFINA
Up to this point. In the still center of your identity.

TEDDY
In the penetralia.

DELFINA
In the innermost places. The hideaways.

TEDDY
The hidey holes.

DELFINA
Day by day. Deepest night. Who were you?

MICHAEL
I don't know what that question means. It's a joke question. The answer's *Boo.* Because there's no considered response that's nearly so apt as babble. How did I live? Out there, in the hard and fast, I devised a kind of glancing man. Picnicked with the

sales managers in the sheep meadow. For my wife, I built a hus-band, contractually bound. Loved and touched. Tossed the salad. But who was I? *Ga ga ga ga ga*. In the seams of being, nobody. In the final spiral strand, nobody, soul-lonely, smoke.

DELFINA
Then what? Tell us. Hurry.

MICHAEL
The toilet began to sway something awful. A rocking and bang-ing. Tremendous turbulent air.

LIVIA
I don't believe any of this. Michael.

MICHAEL
A light began to flash that I could see only blurry through the shroud.

DELFINA
Use the present tense, please.

MICHAEL
I'm bouncing off the toilet walls. Trying to find the handgrip. The pilot's talking on the intercom.

TEDDY
Looks like we're experiencing some real heavy air at this partic-ular point in time.

MICHAEL
I unwind the unwaxed floss. I lift off the shroud and read the urgent flashing light.

TEDDY
Return to seat. Return to seat. Return to seat.

MICHAEL
And I became a docile traveler once again. I had to submit to the systems. They were designed to save my life. And I complied gratefully. Returned to my seat. Fastened my seatbelt.

LIVIA
He is lying through his teeth and eyes.

DELFINA
How do you know?

LIVIA
Suicide? He would have told me.

DELFINA
That's exactly what he's doing. He's telling you. Teddy.

TEDDY
I believe him.

DELFINA
I believe him too.

LIVIA
It never happened. And if it did, it wasn't a real attempt. You can't kill yourself with a plastic bag alone. You have to take pills or booze. Kevorkian gives them vodka.

DELFINA
No, he doesn't. What brand? And besides.

TEDDY
There are video cameras in airline toilets.

DELFINA
The story is verifiable.

TEDDY
The life is verifiable.

MICHAEL
Returned to my seat. Fastened my seatbelt. There were two hours left in the flight.

DELFINA
You invented the legend of Valparaiso.

MICHAEL
The mayor came out to greet me with half his staff.

DELFINA
Wine appeared in long-stemmed glasses.

MICHAEL
Cameramen in baggy pants. We talked and laughed and proposed hemispheric toasts. To Valparaiso.

TEDDY
To all the Valparaisos.

DELFINA
Out of the genius and terror of night. Comes the sky-dancing man in radiant haze. You like that line?

TEDDY
People. Come on. Together.

DELFINA/TEDDY
Out of the genius and terror of night. Comes the sky-dancing man in radiant haze.

MICHAEL
Vivir.

TEDDY

To live.

DELFINA

But it's over now, isn't it? This empty brimful thing. The interviews. The autographs. The lights and mikes. All the sex toys of your transcendence.

Delfina reaches around, placing her hand mike in Michael's crotch. The instrument begins to glow. Michael takes it in both hands and raises it to chest level as if it were an object of some religious consequence.

MICHAEL

I want to grow a beard. I'm learning Spanish on tape. I had a passport.

TEDDY

I had a passport.

DELFINA

What is the word that describes the condition of a man who advances bravely toward his own grueling truth?

TEDDY

Perishability.

DELFINA

A tragic figure finally. O Michael. This is the apex of your experience. Followed of course.

MICHAEL

I sign their flight coupons. Their food coupons. People in long shuffling lines. They have Cadillacs. They have recurring Rivieras. They have grass blades stuck to their shoes. You know how grass. This is something I associate with childhood. The way grass sticks out from under a child's shoe after a day of play. One of those rhyming days of summer when children play on burning lawns and stand in shuffling lines and you can detect the mild sweat, child sweat, nothing like the nasty reek you produce as a man. You know how grass blades bend underfoot. We're a nation of grass. Bluegrass, bermuda grass. All the grasses that begin with the letter *b*. We're blessed with grass. In Saudi Arabia there is no grass. They have to fly it in synthetically. They have Cadillacs. They have sheiks in flowing robes.

DELFINA
What kind of underwear?

MICHAEL
Erotomaniacal.

DELFINA
Melt into me. Michael. Hurry.

MICHAEL
People who take their laptops to the toilet with them. I sign their memory chips. Their bone china. They have osteoporosis. They have early menopause. Great big barbered network executives. I don't differentiate. The plane is taking off outside the cabin and the plane is taking off inside the cabin. Objects in the overhead sometimes shift during flight. I look at the monitor, I look at the earth. Then what. I run. I make up my mind and run. I run senselessly and breathlessly. I run through the terminal toward surface transportation. (*Pause.*) She jerked me off in a taxi once. This is the apex of my experience.

DELFINA
Followed of course by the fall.

MICHAEL
This is how I want to live.

DELFINA
How do you want to die?

MICHAEL
By die you mean.

DELFINA
In the best possible sense. In the sense that nothing is left unseen. Nothing is left unsaid. What is your last living thought? Take us through it, Michael.

Delfina reaches around and takes the hand mike.

MICHAEL
Which camera am I talking to?

TEDDY
Talk to camera two.

MICHAEL
I think of a wish-giving woman in a well-pressed uniform with little silver wings on her titty.

DELFINA
What does she say to you? Tell us everything.

MICHAEL
She says to me.

DELFINA
Passenger X, please present yourself at the podium.

MICHAEL
She has her keyboard and her screen. I want something to pass
between us.

DELFINA
There isn't time.

MICHAEL
Some nuance of human sharing.

DELFINA
What does she say to you? Speak. Tell us.

*Delfina grips him by the hair and eases his head back onto her
shoulder. He does not resist.*

MICHAEL
She says to me.

DELFINA
Why are you going to Chicago if your itinerary says Miami?

*Delfina forces the hand mike down his throat, choking him.
Michael sinks slowly down her body to his knees, head slumped
forward.*

Livia is motionless, staring straight ahead.

Teddy browses in a magazine.

Lights down on set.

*Delfina, spotlighted, lets the body slide to the floor. She steps over
it and faces into camera.*

(*To camera*) Someone dies, remotely known to you, but how real
and deep the loss. Who is he? An image aloft in the flashing air.

Not even that. A set of image-forming units, sand-grain size, that shape a face on-screen. How can it be? A life so unfleshed takes up intimate space. Someone spun of lightwaves and repetitious sounds. How is it possible? This odd soak of gloom heavy in your chest. (*To audience*) We live in the air as well as the skin. And there is something in these grids of information that strikes the common heart as magic.

Spotlight down.

Lights up on Chorus, center stage.

At the first reference to the oxygen mask, the two flanking members mimic the action of drawing the mask toward the face. They do this repeatedly as all three members continue the recitation.

CHORUS
In the event of a drop in cabin pressure
In the unlikely event
Jump onto the slide with legs extended
Passengers in designated exit seats
Then place the mask   Then place the mask
Has anyone had access
Has anyone made an approach
Then place the mask
Passengers in designated exit seats
Please make your selection
Then place the mask   Then place the mask
Has anyone had access
Has anyone told you retroactively
Please make your selection
Then place the mask
In the unlikely event
Jump onto the slide with legs
Has a nondescript individual
Has a man in an unmarked car

Passengers in designated exit seats
In the unlikely event
Please make your selection
Then place the mask   Then place—

The recitation stops abruptly. The two gesturing members freeze in midmotion. Lights slowly down.

A deep pulse of image and sound. Synthesized roaring wind. Videotape of man in confined space with plastic bag on his head. Face obscured.

The tape is projected in a larger format this time. The image spreads over the Chorus and fills the set behind the members. The man's huge shrouded head covers the furniture and bends up the back wall.

The projection lasts fifteen seconds.

Stillness. Then lights up bright on Chorus, flanking members still suspended in midgesture.

BLACK